# Five Silly Nanas!

*Copyright © 2022 by Lisa Lawton, Krystina Thiel-Smalley, and Brent R. Brandmayr*
*All rights reserved.*
*Published in the United States by Brent's Books*

*Brent's Books ® is a registered trademark belonging to Brent's Books*

*Visit us on the Web at*
*www.brentsbooks.com*

*Five Silly Nanas!*
*Summary: Five Silly Nanas go to visit Claire by the sea and have a real adventure!  Claire learns that her*
*Nanas are sillier than ever, and has to put her foot down on their shenanigans when they start getting injured.*
*Written by Lisa Lawton and Krystina Thiel-Smalley*
*Illustrated by Brent Brandmayr*
*ISBN 978-1-7364675-1-0 (trade)*

*Printed in the United States of America*

This Book
Belongs To:

Five silly Nanas driving to the sea,

Visiting their families, happy as can be.

SILLY5

Arriving at the hotel, they called Sweet Claire,

she squealed with Joy, "I'll be right there!"

Knocking on the door of the room by the sea,

she peeked right in and what did she see?

Five silly Nanas jumping on the bed,

One fell off and bumped her head,

Claire called the doctor and the doctor said,

"No more Nanas jumping on the bed!"

Four silly Nanas jumping on the bed,

One fell off and bumped her head,

Claire called the doctor and the doctor said,

"No more Nanas jumping on the bed!"

Three silly Nanas jumping on the bed,

One fell off and bumped her head,

Claire called the doctor and the doctor said,

"No more Nanas jumping on the bed!"

Two silly Nanas jumping on the bed,

One fell off and bumped her head,

Claire called the doctor and the doctor said,

"No more Nanas jumping on the bed!"

One silly Nana jumping on the bed,

She fell off and bumped her head,

Claire called the doctor and the doctor said,

"NO MORE NANAS JUMPING ON THE BED!"

Claire stomped her foot and loudly yelled,

**"THAT'S QUITE ENOUGH!**

Jumping on the bed is much too rough!

You all came to visit me,

Now let's go out and play by the sea!"

Five silly Nanas jumping in the sea,

Dancin' round Claire, as they giggled with glee.

"Ah", said Claire

"I love my Nanas visiting me,

Just the way it was meant to be."

Krystina and Lisa are sisters who love being Nanas. They have been jumping on beds from when they were very young to now, when they are almost, but not quite, in fact eons away from being very old.

Krystina lives in Great Falls, MT and Lisa lives in Bozeman, MT.


Brent R. Brandmayr was born and raised in Marshalltown, Iowa, and attended Loras College in Dubuque, Iowa.  He now lives in Bozeman, Montana with his wife and two boys.  Many years of campfire tales have been the source of inspiration for his books.  He also has a Fine Art degree, which spurred his interest in illustrating the stories.